VOL. 9

HAL•LEONARD®
KEYBOARD
PLAY ALONG™

Elton John
Ballads

D0613749

ISBN 978-1-4234-4307-0

Visit Hal Leonard Online at **www.halleonard.com**

HAL•LEONARD®
CORPORATION
7777 W. BLUEMOUND RD. P.O. BOX 13819
MILWAUKEE, WISCONSIN 53213

CONTENTS

Blue Eyes

Words and Music by Elton John and Gary Osborne

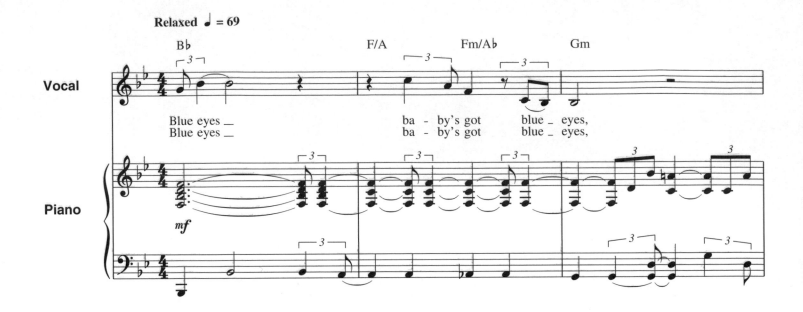

day.
me.
Blue eyes, __
Blue eyes, __

ba - by's got blue __ eyes,
ooh, I love blue __ eyes,
when the morn - ing __
when I'm by __ her __

__ comes, __
__ side __
I'll be far __ a - way, __
where I long __ to be, __

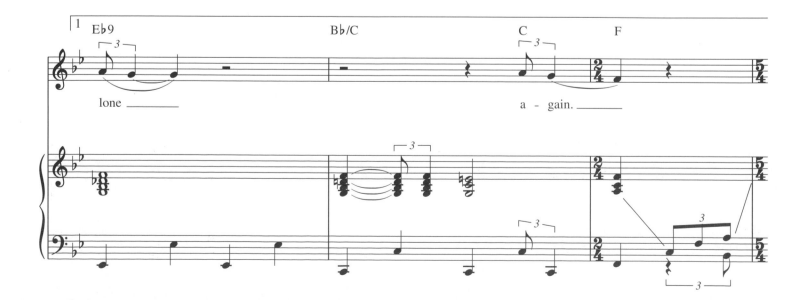

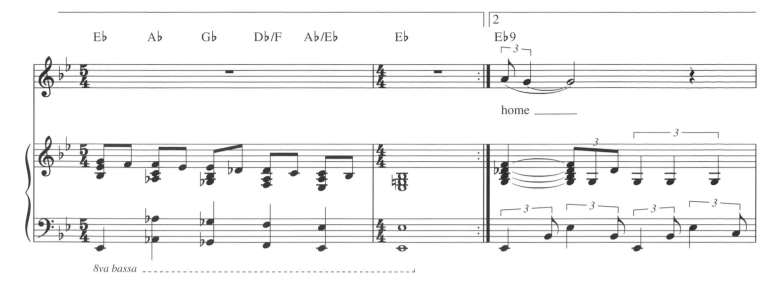

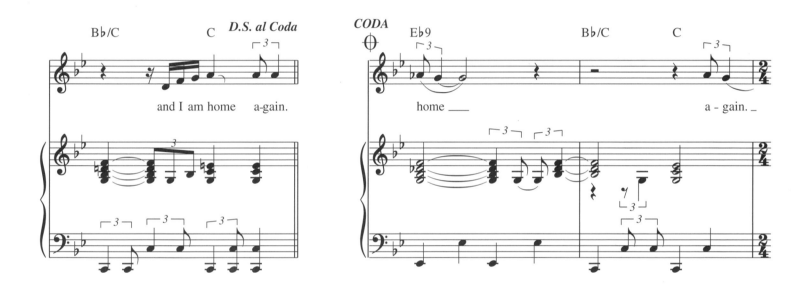

Candle in the Wind

Words and Music by Elton John and Bernie Taupin

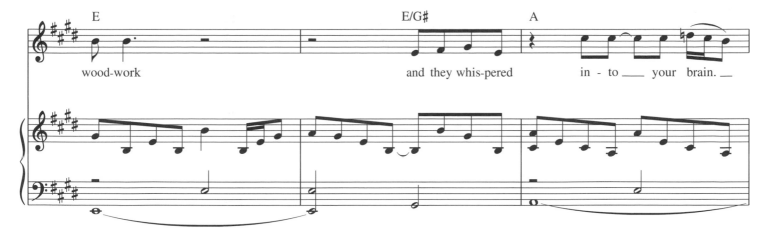

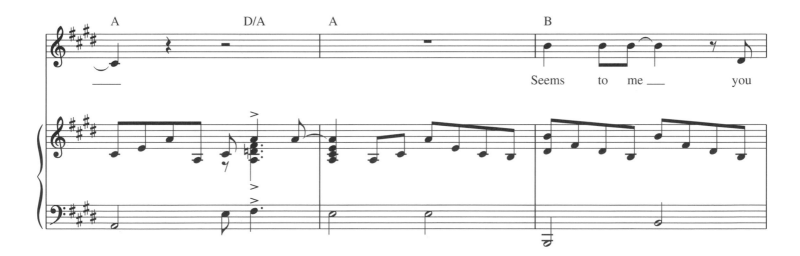

know-ing who to cling __ to when the rain __ set in. __

I would have liked __ to have known you but I was just____

__ a kid. Your can - dle burned __ out long __ be - fore __

your leg - end ev - er did. ____

Lone - li - ness __ was tough, ___ tough-est role you ev - er played. __

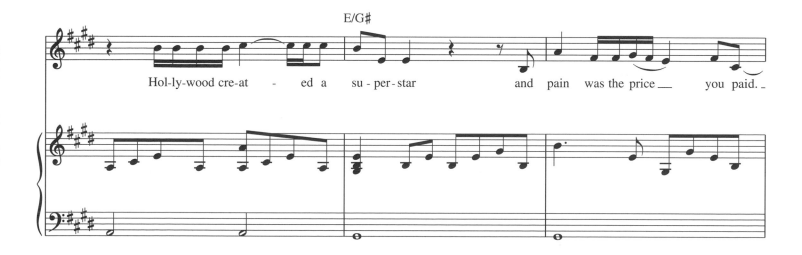

Hol-ly-wood cre-at - ed a su-per-star and pain was the price ___ you paid. __

E - ven when you died, oh, the press ___ still hound - ed you. ___ All the pa - pers had to say ___ was that Mar - i - lyn was found in the nude. ___

Seems to me ___ you lived your life ___ like a

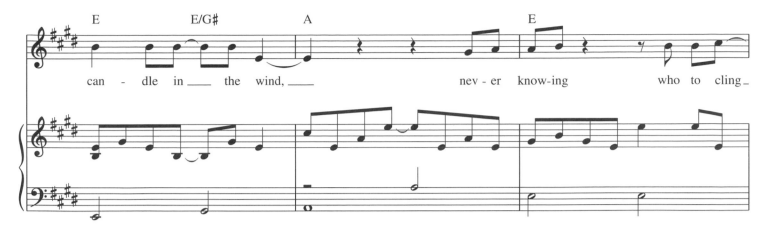

can - dle in ___ the wind, ___ nev - er know-ing who to cling ___

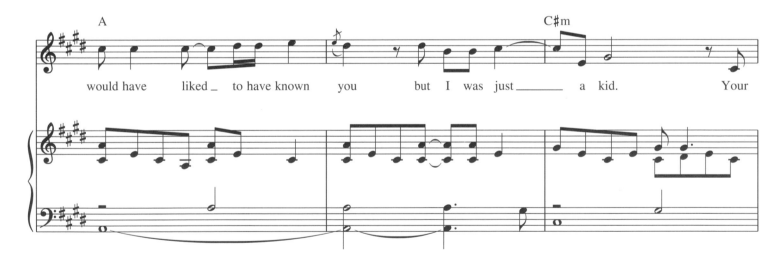

___ to ___ when the rain ___ set in. ___ I

would have liked ___ to have known you but I was just ___ a kid. Your

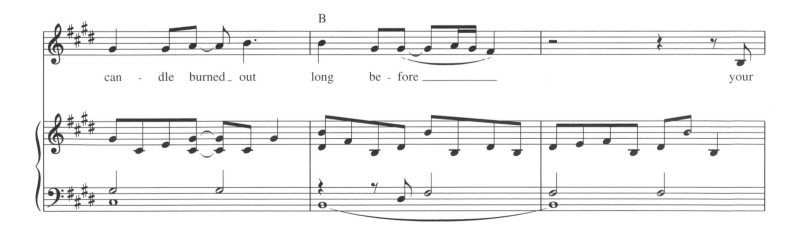

can - dle burned ___ out long be - fore ___ your

leg - end ev - er did. _____

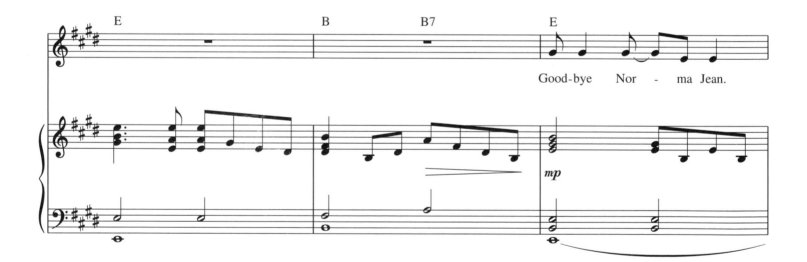

Good-bye Nor - ma Jean.

Though I nev - er knew you __ at all, you had the grace to

Seems to me you lived __ your life __ like a can - dle in __ the wind, __

__ nev - er know - ing who to cling __ to when the rain __

__ set __ in. __ And I would have liked _ to have known

you but I was just _____ a kid. Your can - dle burned _ out

long be-fore _ your leg-end ev-er did. _

I would have liked _ to have known you, oh, _ but I _

_ was just a kid. _____ Your can-dle burned _ out long _ be-fore _

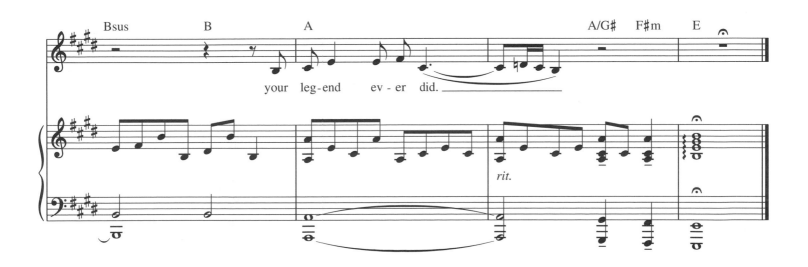

your leg-end ev-er did. _____

Daniel

Words and Music by Elton John and Bernie Taupin

Moderately bright, in 2 ♩ = 66 (Half-time feel)

Dan-iel is trav - 'ling to-night on a plane

19

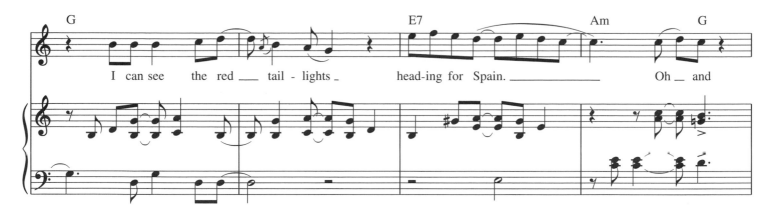

20

They say Spain is pret - ty though I've nev - er been

well Dan-iel says __ it's the best __ place he's ev - er seen. ____ Oh __ and

he should know __ he's been __ there e - nough ____ Lord I __

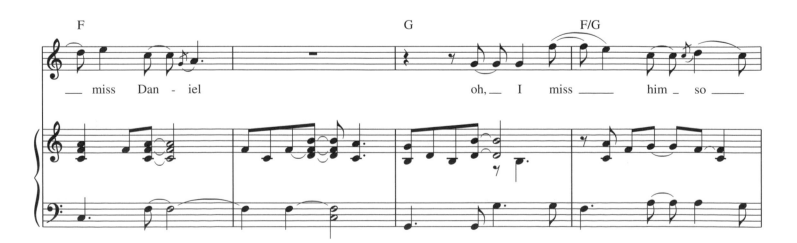

__ miss Dan - iel oh, __ I miss ____ him __ so ____

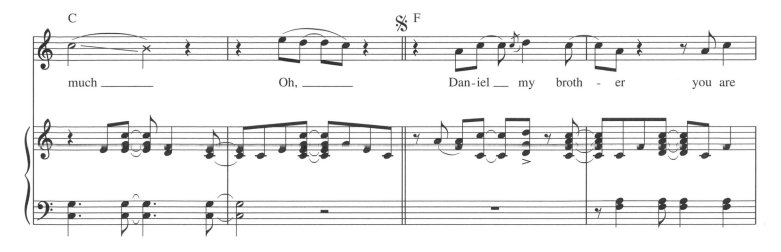

much _____ Oh, _____ Dan-iel ___ my broth - er ___ you are

old - er ___ than _ me ___ do you _ still feel the pain _ of the scars _

___ that _ won't heal. _ Your eyes _ have _ died _____ but you see more _ than _ I. _

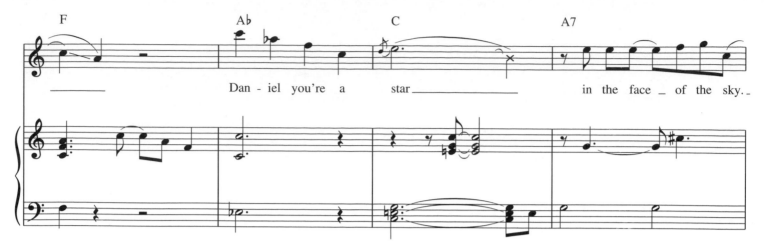

Dan - iel you're a star _____ in the face _ of the sky. _

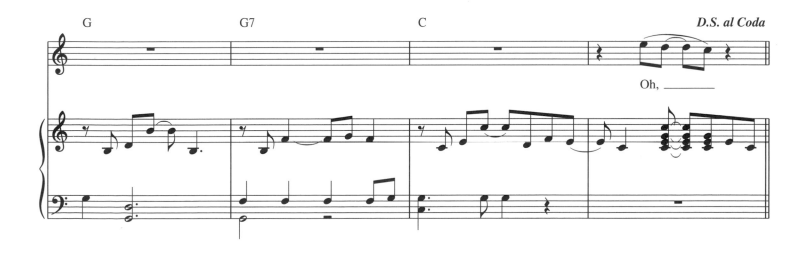

Oh, _____

CODA

Dan-iel is trav - 'ling to-night _ on a plane _

I can see the red __ tail - lights _ head-ing for Spain. __

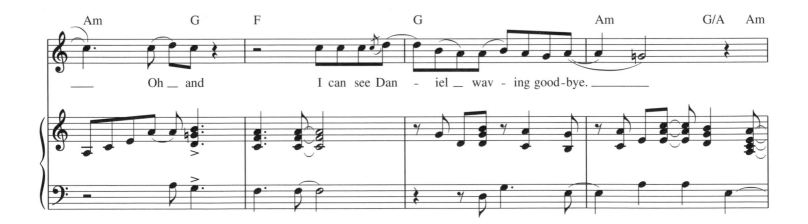

__ Oh __ and I can see Dan - iel _ wav - ing good-bye. __

God it looks _ like Dan - iel must be __ the clouds _

in __ my eyes. ___ Oh God _ it ____ looks like Dan - iel

must be ___ the clouds _____ in ____ my eyes. __

Don't Let the Sun Go Down on Me

Words and Music by Elton John and Bernie Taupin

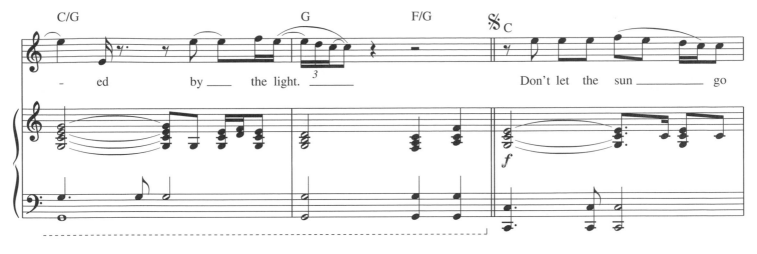
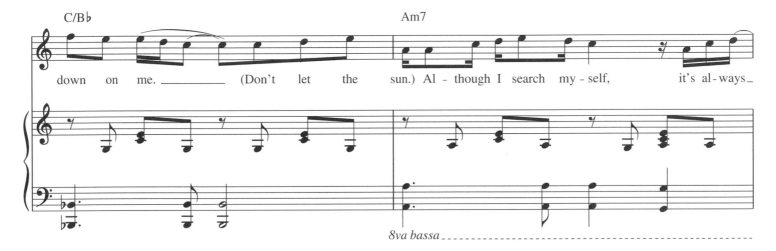
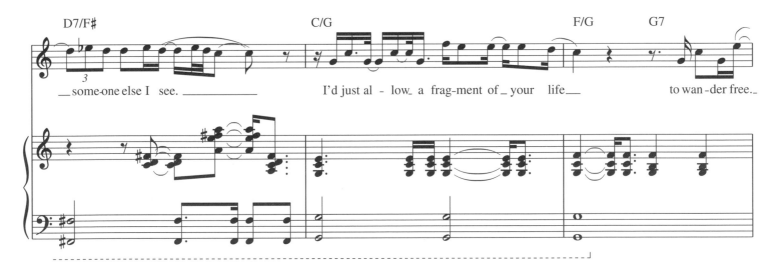

sun go-ing down on me.

I can't find oh the right ro-

man-tic line. But see me once

and see the way I feel.

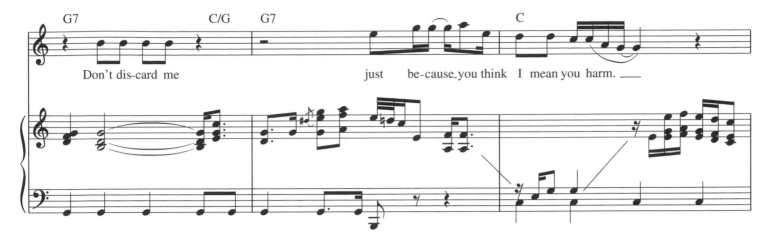

Don't dis-card me   just be-cause you think I mean you harm. _____

But these cuts _ I _ have, _____   oh, they need

8va bassa _ _ _ _ ⌐

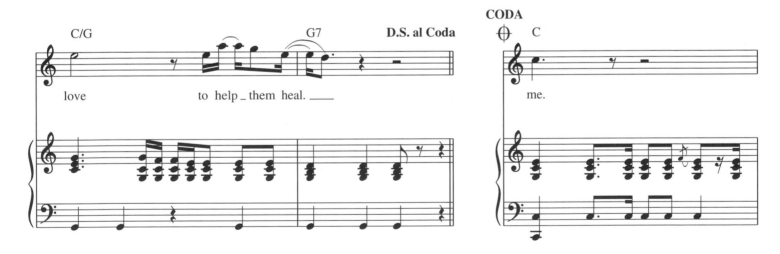

D.S. al Coda   **CODA**

love   to help _ them heal. _____   me.

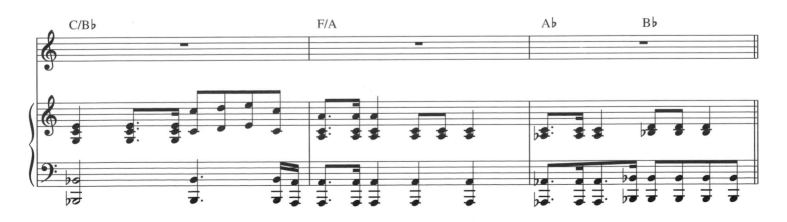

Don't let the sun ___ go down _ on me. _____

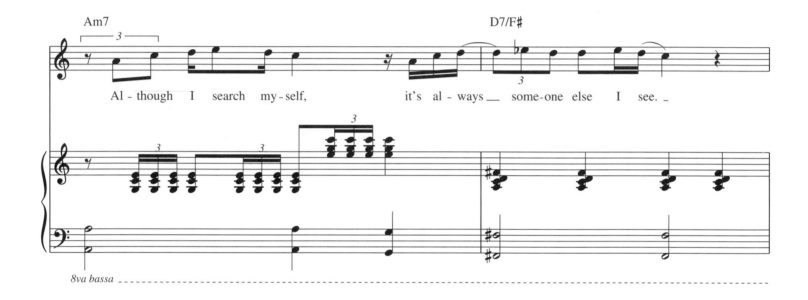

Al - though I search my - self, it's al - ways ___ some-one else I see. _

8va bassa -

I'd just al - low a frag - ment of ___ your life ___ to wan - der free. _

Yeah. But

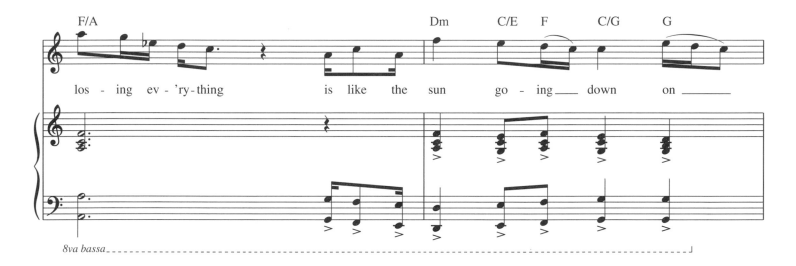

los - ing ev - 'ry-thing is like the sun go - ing___ down on _____

8va bassa

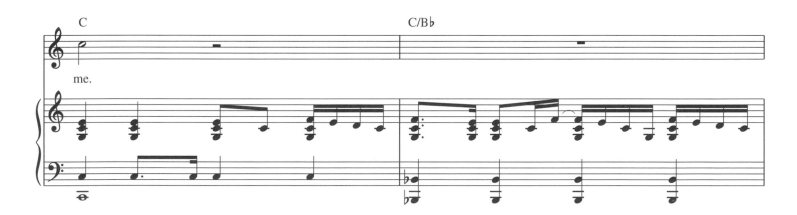

me.

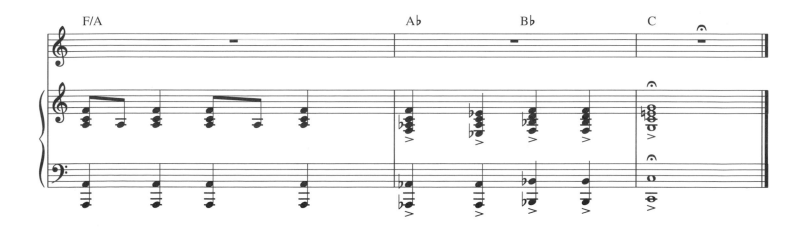

Goodbye Yellow Brick Road

Words and Music by Elton John and Bernie Taupin

know you can't hold __ me for - ev - __ er   I did- n't sign up __ with you. __

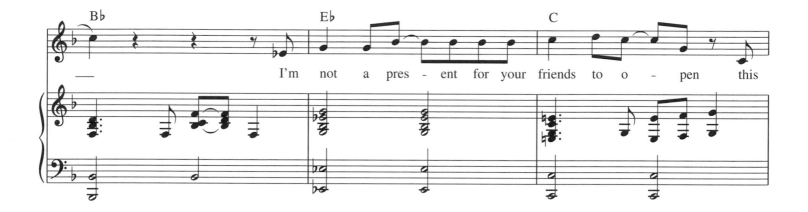

__ I'm not a pres - ent for your friends to o - pen this

boy's too young __ to be sing - ing   the   blues. _____

ground. _____

2nd time sim.

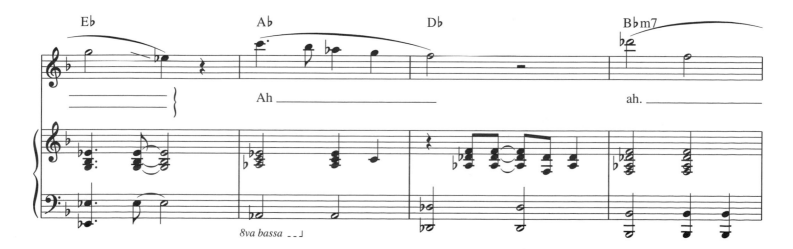

Ah _____   ah. _____

To Coda

yond the yel-low brick road. _____ Ah _____

___ ah _____ ah.

What do you think you'll do _ then I bet they'd shoot down _ the plane. _

___ It-'ll take you a cou-ple of vod-ka and ton-ics to set you on your feet a-gain. _

May-be you'll get_ a re-place - ment there's plen-ty like me_ to be found._

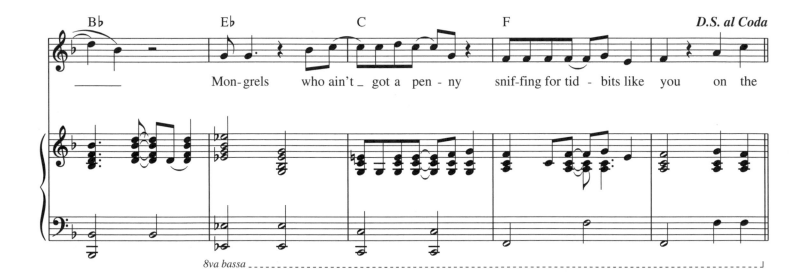

Mon-grels who ain't_ got a pen-ny snif-fing for tid - bits like you on the

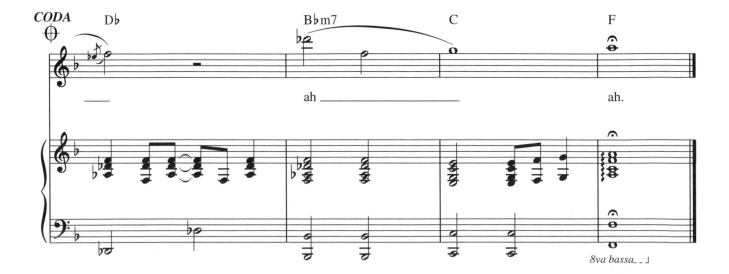

ah _____ ah.

Rocket Man
(I Think It's Gonna Be a Long Long Time)

Words and Music by Elton John and Bernie Taupin

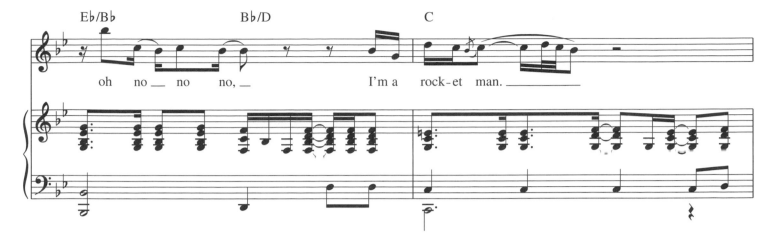

oh no __ no no, __ I'm a rock-et man. __

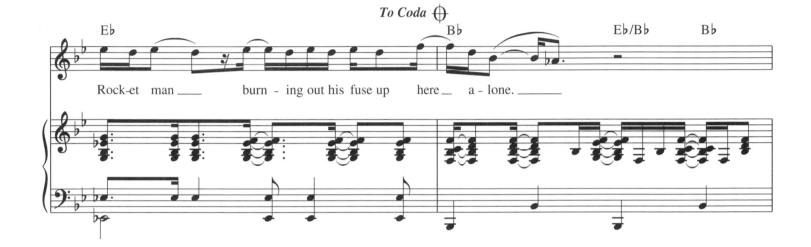

To Coda ⊕

Rock-et man __ burn - ing out his fuse up here __ a - lone. __

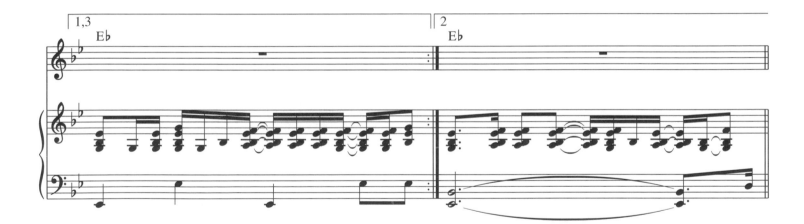

Mars ain't the kind of place __ to raise your kids. __ In fact, __ it's cold __ as hell. __

And there's no one there _ to _ raise _ them if you did. _

And all _ this sci-ence _ I don't un-der-stand. It's just _ my job _ five days a week. _

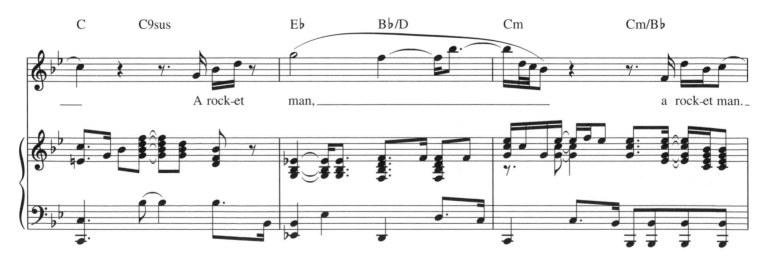

_ A rock-et man, _ a rock-et man. _

D.S. al Coda
(Take first ending)

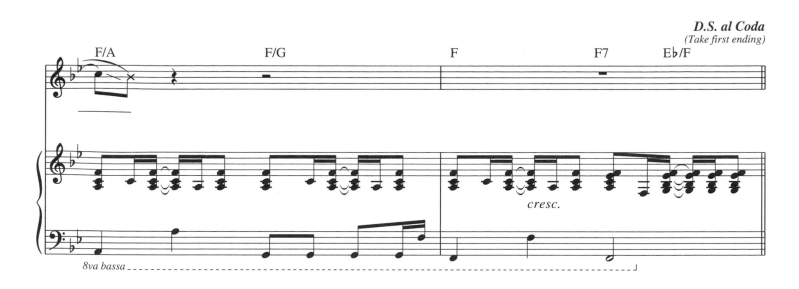

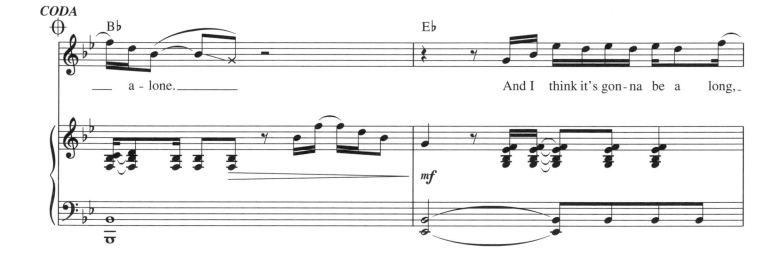

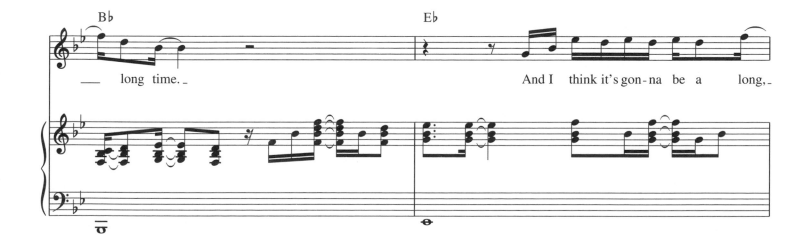

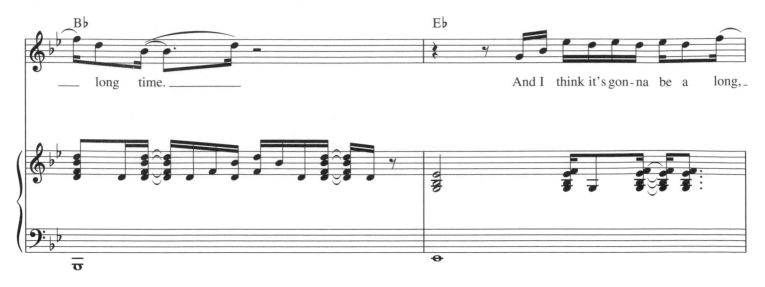

_____ long time. _____

And I think it's gon-na be a   long,_

_____ long time._____

And I think it's gon-na be a   long, long time._

And I   think it's gon-na be a   long, _____ long time._

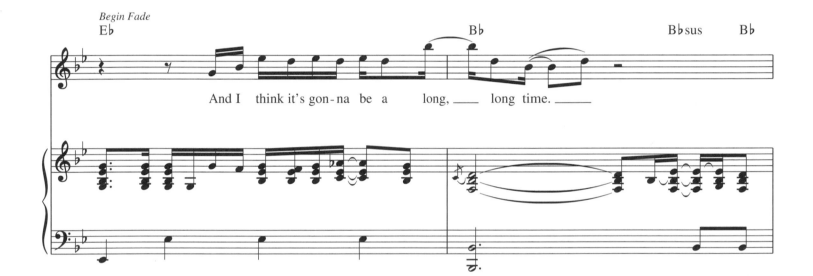

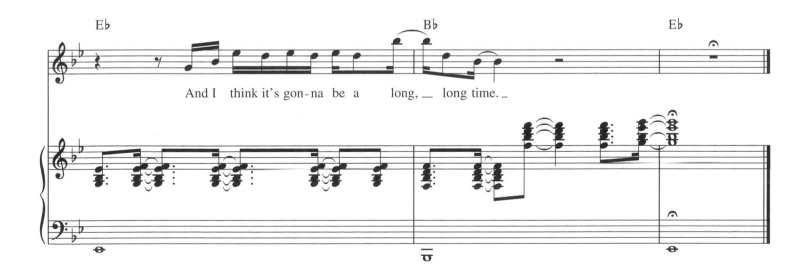

Someone Saved My Life Tonight

Words and Music by Elton John and Bernie Taupin

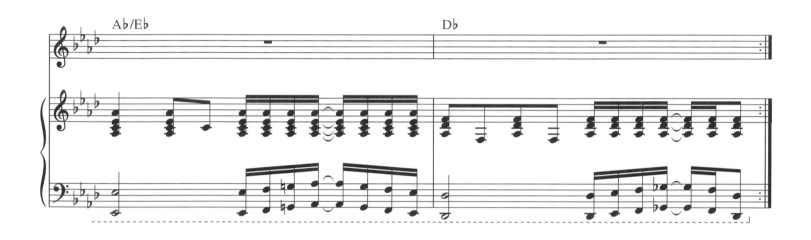

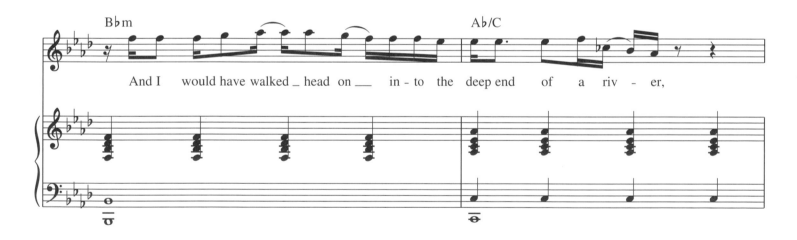

And I would have walked __ head on __ in-to the deep end of a riv - er,

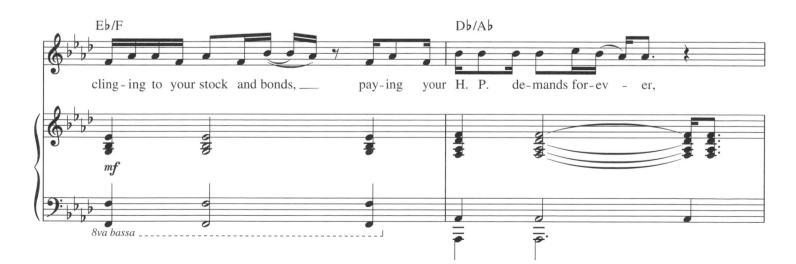

cling-ing to your stock and bonds, ___ pay-ing your H. P. de-mands for-ev - er,

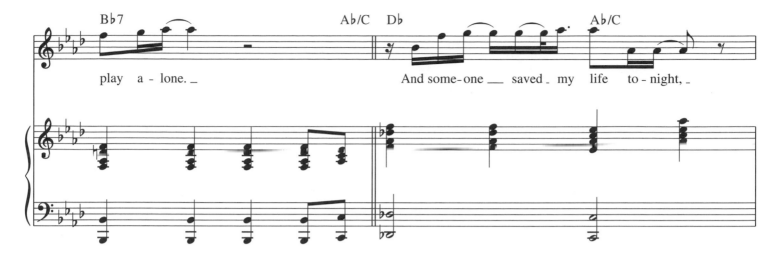

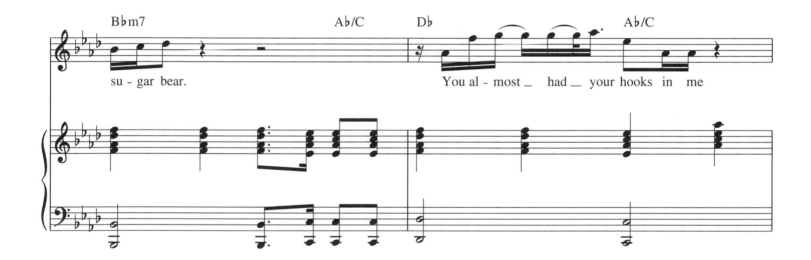

al - tar bound, ___ hyp-no-tized, ___ sweet free - dom whis-pered in ___ my ear. You're a

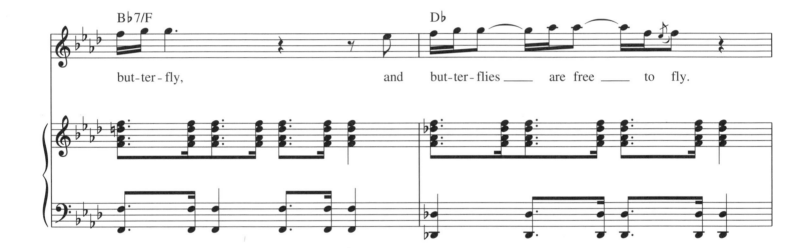

but-ter-fly, and but-ter-flies ___ are free ___ to fly.

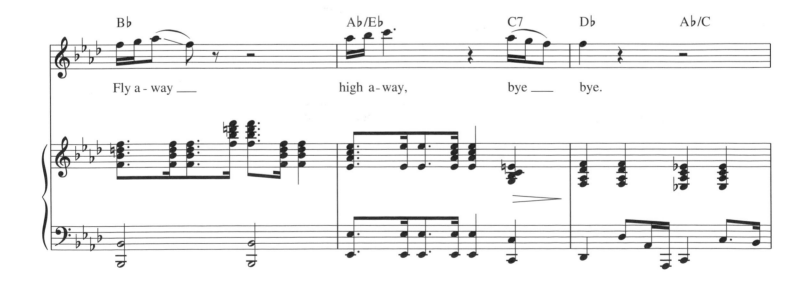

Fly a - way ___ high a-way, bye ___ bye.

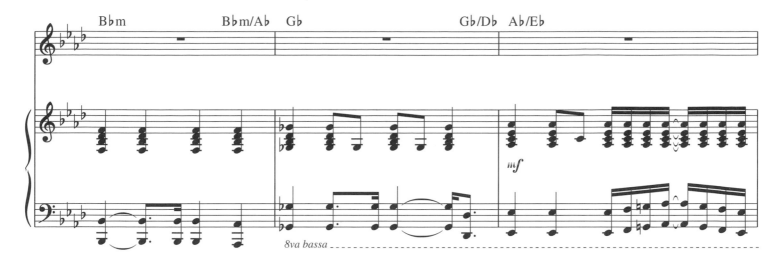

Repeat and Fade

Some-one saved, some-one saved, some-one saved my life ___ to-night.__

Sorry Seems to Be the Hardest Word

Words and Music by Elton John and Bernie Taupin

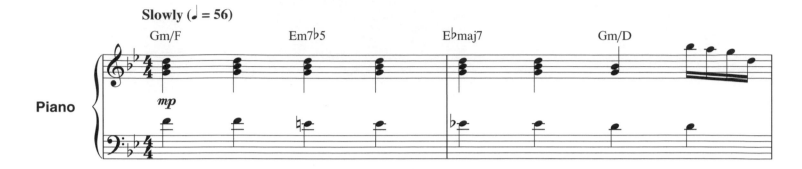

What have I got to do to make you love ___ me?

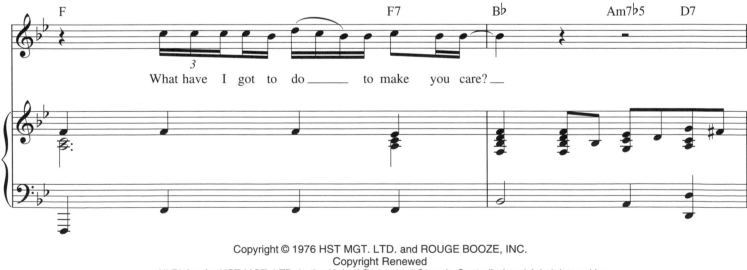

What have I got to do _____ to make you care? ___

What do I say when it's all o - ver? And

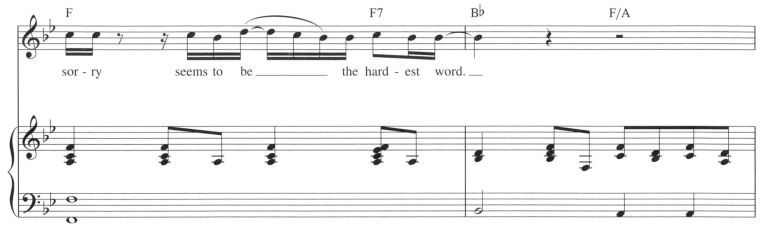

sor - ry seems to be _____ the hard - est word. ____

It's sad, _____ so sad. _____ It's a sad, sad sit - u - a - tion, __

and it's get - ting more and more __ ab - surd. ____

It's so sad, __ so sad. ___ Why can't __ we talk __ it o - ver? ___

Oh, it seems to me ___ that sor - ry seems to be ___ the hard - est word. __

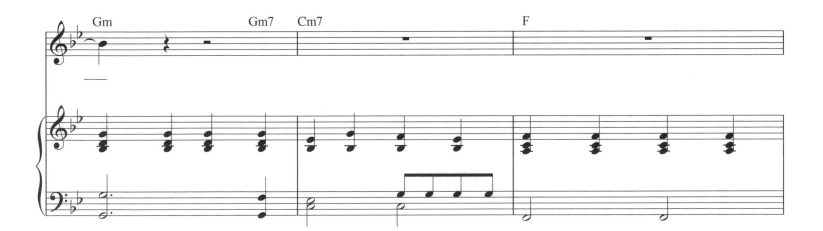

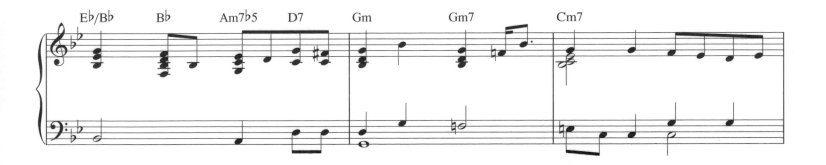

It's sad, _____ so sad. _____ It's a sad, sad sit - u - a - tion, _____

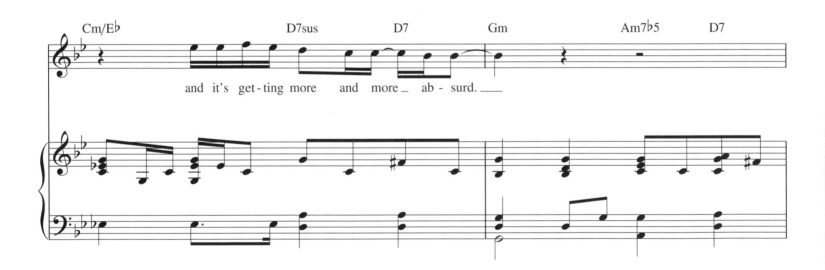

and it's get-ting more and more _ ab - surd. _____

It's so sad, _ so sad. _____ Why can't _ we talk _ it o - ver? _____

Oh, it seems to me ___ that sor - ry seems to be ___ the hard - est

word. ___ What do I do to make you love ___ me?

What have I got to do ___ to be heard? ___

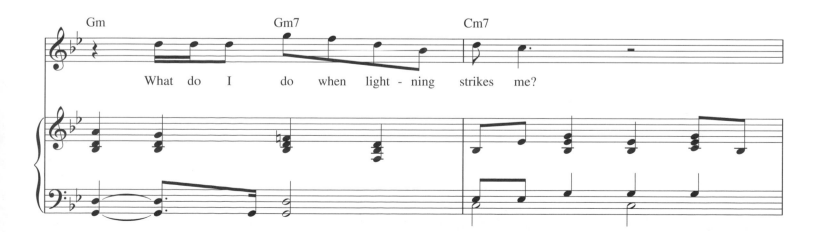

What do I do when light - ning strikes me?

What have I got to do, __ What have I got to do _____ when

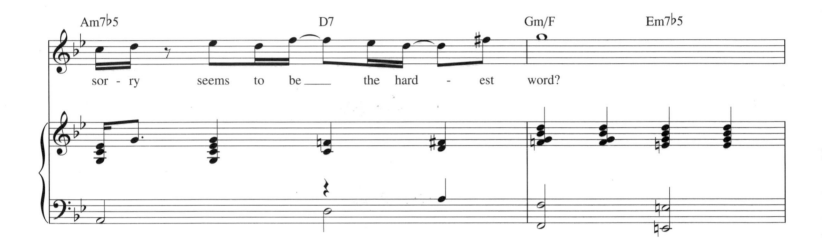

sor - ry seems to be ____ the hard - est word?

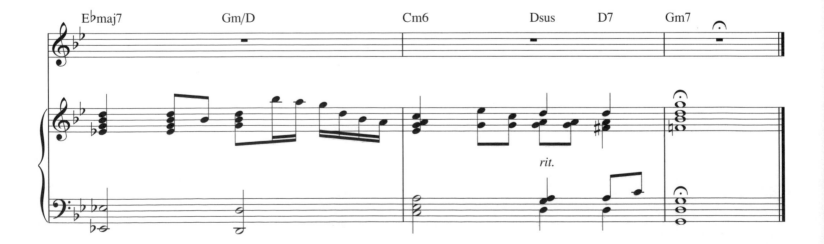

rit.

HAL•LEONARD KEYBOARD PLAY-ALONG

The Keyboard Play-Along series will help you quickly and easily play your favorite songs as played by your favorite artists. Just follow the music in the book, listen to the CD to hear how the keyboard should sound, and then play along using the separate backing tracks. The melody and lyrics are also included in the book in case you want to sing, or simply to help you follow along. The audio CD is playable on any CD player. For PC and Mac users, the CD is enhanced so you can adjust the recording to any tempo without changing pitch! Each book/ CD pack in this series features eight great songs.

1. POP/ROCK HITS

Against All Odds (Take a Look at Me Now) (Phil Collins) • Deacon Blues (Steely Dan) • (Everything I Do) I Do It for You (Bryan Adams) • Hard to Say I'm Sorry (Chicago) • Kiss on My List (Hall & Oates) • My Life (Billy Joel) • Walking in Memphis (Marc Cohn) • What a Fool Believes (The Doobie Brothers).
00699875 Keyboard Transcriptions $14.95

2. SOFT ROCK

Don't Know Much (Aaron Neville) • Glory of Love (Peter Cetera) • I Write the Songs (Barry Manilow) • It's Too Late (Carole King) • Just Once (James Ingram) • Making Love Out of Nothing at All (Air Supply) • We've Only Just Begun (Carpenters) • You Are the Sunshine of My Life (Stevie Wonder).
00699876 Keyboard Transcriptions $12.95

3. CLASSIC ROCK

Against the Wind (Bob Seger) • Come Sail Away (Styx) • Don't Do Me like That (Tom Petty and the Heartbreakers) • Jessica (Allman Brothers) • Say You Love Me (Fleetwood Mac) • Takin' Care of Business (Bachman-Turner Overdrive) • Werewolves of London (Warren Zevon) • You're My Best Friend (Queen).
00699877 Keyboard Transcriptions $14.95

4. CONTEMPORARY ROCK

Angel (Sarah McLachlan) • Beautiful (Christina Aguilera) • Because of You (Kelly Clarkson) • Don't Know Why (Norah Jones) • Fallin' (Alicia Keys) • Listen to Your Heart (D.H.T.) • A Thousand Miles (Vanessa Carlton) • Unfaithful (Rihanna).
00699878 Keyboard Transcriptions $12.95

5. ROCK HITS

Back at One (Brian McKnight) • Brick (Ben Folds) • Clocks (Coldplay) • Drops of Jupiter (Tell Me) (Train) • Home (Michael Buble) • 100 Years (Five for Fighting) • This Love (Maroon 5) • You're Beautiful (James Blunt)
00699879 Keyboard Transcriptions $14.95

6. ROCK BALLADS

Bridge over Troubled Water (Simon & Garfunkel) • Easy (Commodores) • Hey Jude (Beatles) • Imagine (John Lennon) • Maybe I'm Amazed (Paul McCartney) • A Whiter Shade of Pale (Procol Harum) • You Are So Beautiful (Joe Cocker) • Your Song (Elton John).
00699880 Keyboard Transcriptions $14.95

7. ROCK CLASSICS

Baba O'Riley (The Who) • Bloody Well Right (Supertramp) • Carry on Wayward Son (Kansas) • Changes (David Bowie) • Cold As Ice (Foreigner) • Evil Woman (Electric Light Orchestra) • Space Truckin' (Deep Purple) • That's All (Genesis).
00699881 Keyboard Transcriptions $14.95

11. THE DOORS

Break on Through to the Other Side • Hello, I Love You (Won't You Tell Me Your Name?) • L.A. Woman • Light My Fire • Love Me Two Times • People Are Strange • Riders on the Storm • Roadhouse Blues.
00699886 Keyboard Transcriptions $14.95

12. CHRISTMAS HITS

Baby, It's Cold Outside (Tom Jones & Cerys Matthews) • Blue Christmas (Elvis Presley) • Merry Christmas, Darling (Carpenters) • Mistletoe and Wine (Cliff Richard) • Santa Baby (Eartha Kitt) • A Spaceman Came Travelling (Chris de Burgh) • Step into Christmas (Elton John) • Wonderful Christmastime (Paul McCartney).
00700267 Keyboard Transcriptions $14.95

Prices, contents, and availability subject to change without notice.

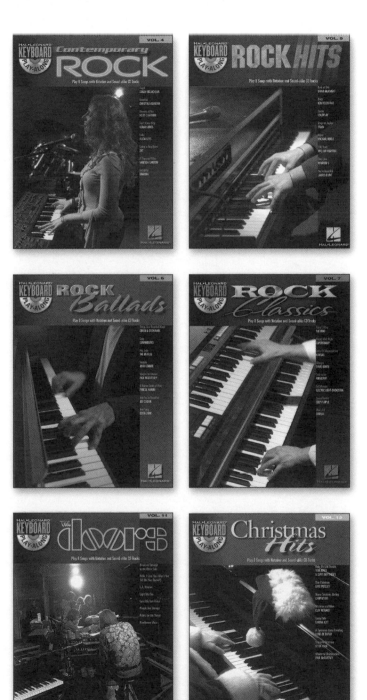

FOR MORE INFORMATION,
SEE YOUR LOCAL MUSIC DEALER,
OR WRITE TO:

HAL•LEONARD®
CORPORATION
7777 W. BLUEMOUND RD. P.O. BOX 13819
MILWAUKEE, WISCONSIN 53213

NOTE-FOR-NOTE
KEYBOARD TRANSCRIPTIONS

These outstanding collections feature note-for-note transcriptions from the artists who made the songs famous. No matter what style you play, these books are perfect for performers or students who want to play just like their keyboard idols.

ACOUSTIC PIANO BALLADS

16 acoustic piano favorites: Angel • Candle in the Wind • Don't Let the Sun Go Down on Me • Endless Love • Imagine • It's Too Late • Let It Be • Mandy • Ribbon in the Sky • Sailing • She's Got a Way • So Far Away • Tapestry • You Never Give Me Your Money • You've Got a Friend • Your Song.
00690351 ....$19.95

ELTON JOHN

18 of Elton John's best songs: Bennie and the Jets • Candle in the Wind • Crocodile Rock • Daniel • Don't Let the Sun Go Down on Me • Goodbye Yellow Brick Road • I Guess That's Why They Call It the Blues • Little Jeannie • Rocket Man • Your Song • and more.
00694829 ....$20.95

THE BEATLES KEYBOARD BOOK

23 Beatles favorites, including: All You Need Is Love • Back in the U.S.S.R. • Come Together • Get Back • Good Day Sunshine • Hey Jude • Lady Madonna • Let It Be • Lucy in the Sky with Diamonds • Ob-La-Di, Ob-La-Da • Oh! Darling • Penny Lane • Revolution • We Can Work It Out • With a Little Help from My Friends • and more.
00694827 ....$22.95

THE CAROLE KING KEYBOARD BOOK

16 of King's greatest songs: Beautiful • Been to Canaan • Home Again • I Feel the Earth Move • It's Too Late • Jazzman • (You Make Me Feel) Like a Natural Woman • Nightingale • Smackwater Jack • So Far Away • Sweet Seasons • Tapestry • Way Over Yonder • Where You Lead • Will You Love Me Tomorrow • You've Got a Friend.
00690554 ....$19.95

CLASSIC ROCK

35 all-time rock classics: Beth • Bloody Well Right • Changes • Cold as Ice • Come Sail Away • Don't Do Me like That • Hard to Handle • Heaven • Killer Queen • King of Pain • Layla • Light My Fire • Oye Como Va • Piano Man • Takin' Care of Business • Werewolves of London • and more.
00310940 ....$24.95

POP/ROCK

35 songs, including: Africa • Against All Odds • Axel F • Centerfold • Chariots of Fire • Cherish • Don't Let the Sun Go Down on Me • Drops of Jupiter (Tell Me) • Faithfully • It's Too Late • Just the Way You Are • Let It Be • Mandy • Sailing • Sweet Dreams Are Made of This • Walking in Memphis • and more.
00310939 ....$24.95

JAZZ

24 favorites from Bill Evans, Thelonious Monk, Oscar Peterson, Bud Powell, Art Tatum and more. Includes: Ain't Misbehavin' • April in Paris • Autumn in New York • Body and Soul • Freddie Freeloader • Giant Steps • My Funny Valentine • Satin Doll • Song for My Father • Stella by Starlight • and more.
00310941 ....$22.95

R&B

35 R&B classics: Baby Love • Boogie on Reggae Woman • Easy • Endless Love • Fallin' • Green Onions • Higher Ground • I'll Be There • Just Once • Money (That's What I Want) • On the Wings of Love • Ribbon in the Sky • This Masquerade • Three Times a Lady • and more.
00310942 ....$24.95

JAZZ STANDARDS

23 classics by 23 jazz masters, including: Blue Skies • Come Rain or Come Shine • Honeysuckle Rose • I Remember You • A Night in Tunisia • Stormy Weather (Keeps Rainin' All the Time) • Where or When • and more.
00311731 ....$22.95

STEVIE WONDER

14 of Stevie's most popular songs: Boogie on Reggae Woman • Hey Love • Higher Ground • I Wish • Isn't She Lovely • Lately • Living for the City • Overjoyed • Ribbon in the Sky • Send One Your Love • Superstition • That Girl • You Are the Sunshine of My Life • You Haven't Done Nothin'.
00306698 ....$21.95

THE BILLY JOEL KEYBOARD BOOK

16 mega-hits from the Piano Man himself: Allentown • And So It Goes • Honesty • Just the Way You Are • Movin' Out • My Life • New York State of Mind • Piano Man • Pressure • She's Got a Way • Tell Her About It • and more.
00694828 ....$22.95

Prices, contents and availability subject to change without notice.

FOR MORE INFORMATION, SEE YOUR LOCAL MUSIC DEALER,
OR WRITE TO:

HAL•LEONARD®
CORPORATION
7777 W. BLUEMOUND RD. P.O. BOX 13819 MILWAUKEE, WI 53213

Visit Hal Leonard online at **www.halleonard.com**

0209

THE ULTIMATE SONGBOOKS

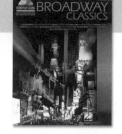

These great songbook/CD packs come with our standard arrangements for piano and voice with guitar chord frames plus a CD.
The CD includes a full performance of each song, as well as a second track without the piano part so you can play "lead" with the band!

1. Movie Music
Come What May • My Heart Will Go On (Love Theme from *Titanic*) • The Rainbow Connection • and more.
00311072 P/V/G......................$14.95

2. Jazz Ballads
Georgia on My Mind • In a Sentimental Mood • The Nearness of You • The Very Thought of You • When Sunny Gets Blue • and more.
00311073 P/V/G......................$14.95

3. Timeless Pop
Ebony and Ivory • Every Breath You Take • From a Distance • I Write the Songs • In My Room • Let It Be • Oh, Pretty Woman • We've Only Just Begun.
00311074 P/V/G......................$14.95

4. Broadway Classics
Ain't Misbehavin' • Cabaret • If I Were a Bell • Memory • Oklahoma • Some Enchanted Evening • The Sound of Music • You'll Never Walk Alone.
00311075 P/V/G......................$14.95

5. Disney
Beauty and the Beast • Can You Feel the Love Tonight • A Whole New World • You'll Be in My Heart • You've Got a Friend in Me • and more.
00311076 P/V/G......................$14.95

6. Country Standards
Blue Eyes Crying in the Rain • Crazy • King of the Road • Oh, Lonesome Me • Ring of Fire • Tennessee Waltz • You Are My Sunshine • Your Cheatin' Heart.
00311077 P/V/G......................$14.95

7. Love Songs
Can't Help Falling in Love • Here, There and Everywhere • How Deep Is Your Love • Maybe I'm Amazed • You Are So Beautiful • and more.
00311078 P/V/G......................$14.95

8. Classical Themes
Can Can • Habanera • Humoresque • In the Hall of the Mountain King • Minuet in G Major • Symphony No. 5 in C Minor, 1st Movement Excerpt • and more.
00311079 Piano Solo......................$14.95

9. Children's Songs
Do-Re-Mi • It's a Small World • Linus and Lucy • Sesame Street Theme • Sing • Winnie the Pooh • Won't You Be My Neighbor? • Yellow Submarine.
0311080 P/V/G......................$14.95

10. Wedding Classics
Air on the G String • Ave Maria • Bridal Chorus • Canon in D • Jesu, Joy of Man's Desiring • Ode to Joy • Trumpet Voluntary • Wedding March.
00311081 Piano Solo......................$14.95

11. Wedding Favorites
All I Ask of You • Don't Know Much • Endless Love • Grow Old with Me • In My Life • Longer • Wedding Processional • You and I.
00311097 P/V/G......................$14.95

12. Christmas Favorites
Blue Christmas • The Christmas Song • Do You Hear What I Hear • Here Comes Santa Claus • Merry Christmas, Darling • Silver Bells • and more.
00311137 P/V/G......................$15.95

13. Yuletide Favorites
Away in a Manger • Deck the Hall • The First Noel • Go, Tell It on the Mountain • Jingle Bells • Joy to the World • O Little Town of Bethlehem • and more.
00311138 P/V/G......................$14.95

14. Pop Ballads
Have I Told You Lately • I'll Be There for You • Rainy Days and Monday • She's Got a Way • Your Song • and more.
00311145 P/V/G......................$14.95

15. Favorite Standards
Call Me • The Girl from Ipanema • Moon River • My Way • Satin Doll • Smoke Gets in Your Eyes • Strangers in the Night • The Way You Look Tonight.
00311146 P/V/G......................$14.95

16. TV Classics
The Brady Bunch • Green Acres Theme • Happy Days • Johnny's Theme • Love Boat Theme • Mister Ed • The Munsters Theme • Where Everybody Knows Your Name.
00311147 P/V/G......................$14.95

17. Movie Favorites
Back to the Future • Theme from *E.T.* • Footloose • Somewhere in Time • Somewhere Out There • and more.
00311148 P/V/G......................$14.95

18. Jazz Standards
All the Things You Are • Bluesette • Easy Living • I'll Remember April • Isn't It Romantic? • Stella by Starlight • Tangerine • Yesterdays.
00311149 P/V/G......................$14.95

19. Contemporary Hits
Beautiful • Calling All Angels • Don't Know Why • If I Ain't Got You • 100 Years • This Love • A Thousand Miles • You Raise Me Up.
00311162 P/V/G......................$14.95

20. R&B Ballads
After the Love Has Gone • All in Love Is Fair • Hello • I'll Be There • Let's Stay Together • Midnight Train to Georgia • Tell It like It Is • Three Times a Lady.
00311163 P/V/G......................$14.95

21. Big Band
All or Nothing at All • Apple Honey • April in Paris • Cherokee • In the Mood • Opus One • Stardust • Stompin' at the Savoy.
00311164 P/V/G......................$14.95

22. Rock Classics
Against All Odds • Bennie and the Jets • Come Sail Away • Do It Again • Free Bird • Jump • Wanted Dead or Alive • We Are the Champions.
00311165 P/V/G......................$14.95

23. Worship Classics
Awesome God • Lord, Be Glorified • Lord, I Lift Your Name on High • Shine, Jesus, Shine • Step by Step • There Is a Redeemer • and more.
00311166 P/V/G......................$14.95

24. Les Misérables
Bring Him Home • Castle on a Cloud • Empty Chairs at Empty Tables • I Dreamed a Dream • A Little Fall of Rain • On My Own • and more.
00311169 P/V/G......................$14.95

25. The Sound of Music
Climb Ev'ry Mountain • Do-Re-Mi • Edelweiss • Maria • My Favorite Things • Sixteen Going on Seventeen • Something Good • The Sound of Music.
00311175 P/V/G......................$15.99

26. Andrew Lloyd Webber Favorites
All I Ask of You • Amigos Para Siempre • As If We Never Said Goodbye • Everything's Alright • Memory • No Matter What • Tell Me on a Sunday • You Must Love Me.
00311178 P/V/G......................$14.95

27. Andrew Lloyd Webber Greats
Don't Cry for Me Argentina • I Don't Know How to Love Him • The Phantom of the Opera • Whistle down the Wind • With One Look • and more.
00311179 P/V/G......................$14.95

28. Lennon & McCartney
Eleanor Rigby • Hey Jude • The Long and Winding Road • Love Me Do • Lucy in the Sky with Diamonds • Nowhere Man • Strawberry Fields Forever • Yesterday.
00311180 P/V/G......................$14.95

29. The Beach Boys
Barbara Ann • Be True to Your School • California Girls • Fun, Fun, Fun • Help Me Rhonda • I Get Around • Little Deuce Coupe • Wouldn't It Be Nice.
00311181 P/V/G......................$14.95

30. Elton John
Candle in the Wind • Crocodile Rock • Daniel • Goodbye Yellow Brick Road • I Guess That's Why They Call It the Blues • Levon • Your Song • and more.
00311182 P/V/G......................$14.95

31. Carpenters
(They Long to Be) Close to You • Only Yesterday • Rainy Days and Mondays • Top of the World • We've Only Just Begun • Yesterday Once More • and more.
00311183 P/V/G......................$14.95

32. Bacharach & David
Alfie • Do You Know the Way to San Jose • The Look of Love • Raindrops Keep Fallin' on My Head • What the World Needs Now Is Love • and more.
00311218 P/V/G......................$14.95

33. Peanuts™
Blue Charlie Brown • Charlie Brown Theme • The Great Pumpkin Waltz • Joe Cool • Linus and Lucy • Oh, Good Grief • Red Baron • You're in Love, Charlie Brown.
00311227 P/V/G......................$14.95

34 Charlie Brown Christmas
Christmas Is Coming • The Christmas Song • Christmas Time Is Here • Linus and Lucy • My Little Drum • O Tannenbaum • Skating • What Child Is This.
00311228 P/V/G......................$15.95

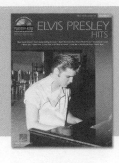

35. Elvis Presley Hits
Blue Suede Shoes • Can't Help Falling in Love • Heartbreak Hotel • Love Me • (Let Me Be Your) Teddy Bear and more.
00311230 P/V/G.............................. $14.95

36. Elvis Presley Greats
All Shook Up • Don't • Jailhouse Rock • Love Me Tender • Loving You • Return to Sender • Too Much • Wooden Heart.
00311231 P/V/G.............................. $14.95

37. Contemporary Christian
El Shaddai • Every Season • Here I Am • Jesus Will Still Be There • Let Us Pray • Place in This World • Who Am I • Wisdom.
00311232 P/V/G.............................. $14.95

38. Duke Ellington Standards
Caravan • I Got It Bad and That Ain't Good • In a Sentimental Mood • Love You Madly • Mood Indigo • Sophisticated Lady • more.
00311233 P/V/G.............................. $14.95

39. Duke Ellington Classics
Don't Get Around Much Anymore • I Let a Song Go out of My Heart • In a Mellow Tone • Satin Doll • Take the "A" Train • and more.
00311234 P/V/G.............................. $14.95

40. Showtunes
The Best of Times • Hello, Dolly! • I'll Know • Mame • Summer Nights • Till There Was You • Tomorrow • What I Did for Love.
00311237 P/V/G.............................. $14.95

41. Rodgers & Hammerstein
Bali Ha'i • Hello, Young Lovers • If I Loved You • It Might as Well Be Spring • Love, Look Away • Oh, What a Beautiful Mornin' • and more.
00311238 P/V/G.............................. $14.95

42. Irving Berlin
Always • Blue Skies • Change Partners • Cheek to Cheek • Easter Parade • How Deep Is the Ocean (How High Is the Sky) • Puttin' on the Ritz • What'll I Do?
00311239 P/V/G.............................. $14.95

43. Jerome Kern
Can't Help Lovin' Dat Man • A Fine Romance • I Won't Dance • I'm Old Fashioned • The Last Time I Saw Paris • Ol' Man River • and more.
00311240 P/V/G.............................. $14.95

44. Frank Sinatra – Popular Hits
Come Fly with Me • Cycles • High Hopes • Love and Marriage • My Way • Strangers in the Night • (Love Is) The Tender Trap • Young at Heart.
00311277 P/V/G.............................. $14.95

45. Frank Sinatra – Most Requested Songs
From Here to Eternity • I've Got the World on a String • Theme from "New York, New York" • Night and Day • Time After Time • Witchcraft • and more.
00311278 P/V/G.............................. $14.95

46. Wicked
Dancing Through Life • Defying Gravity • For Good • I Couldn't Be Happier • I'm Not That Girl • Popular • What Is This Feeling? • The Wizard and I.
00311317 P/V/G.............................. $15.99

47. Rent
I'll Cover You • Light My Candle • One Song Glory • Out Tonight • Rent • Seasons of Love • What You Own • Without You.
00311319 P/V/G.............................. $14.95

48. Christmas Carols
God Rest Ye Merry, Gentlemen • Hark! the Herald Angels Sing • It Came upon the Midnight Clear • O Holy Night • Silent Night • What Child Is This? • and more.
00311332 P/V/G.............................. $14.95

49. Holiday Hits
Frosty the Snow Man • Happy Xmas (War Is Over) • I'll Be Home for Christmas • Jingle-Bell Rock • Rudolph the Red-Nosed Reindeer • Santa Claus Is Comin' to Town • and more.
00311333 P/V/G.............................. $14.95

50. Disney Classics
Some Day My Prince Will Come • When You Wish upon a Star • Whistle While You Work • Who's Afraid of the Big Bad Wolf? • Zip-A-Dee-Doo-Dah • and more.
00311417 P/V/G.............................. $14.95

51. High School Musical
9 songs, including: Breaking Free • Get'cha Head in the Game • Start of Something New • We're All in This Together • What I've Been Looking For • and more.
00311421 P/V/G.............................. $19.95

52. Andrew Lloyd Webber Classics
Another Suitcase in Another Hall • Close Every Door • Love Changes Everything • The Perfect Year • Pie Jesu • Wishing You Were Somehow Here Again • and more.
00311422 P/V/G.............................. $14.95

53. Grease
Beauty School Dropout • Grease • Greased Lightnin' • Hopelessly Devoted to You • Sandy • Summer Nights • You're the One That I Want • and more.
00311450 P/V/G.............................. $14.95

54. Broadway Favorites
Big Spender • Comedy Tonight • Hello, Young Lovers • I've Grown Accustomed to Her Face • Just in Time • Make Someone Happy • My Ship • People.
00311451 P/V/G.............................. $14.95

55. The 1940s
Come Rain or Come Shine • It Could Happen to You • Moonlight in Vermont • A Nightingale Sang in Berkeley Square • Route 66 • Sentimental Journey • and more.
00311453 P/V/G.............................. $14.95

56. The 1950s
Blueberry Hill • Dream Lover • Fever • The Great Pretender • Kansas City • Memories Are Made of This • My Prayer • Put Your Head on My Shoulder.
00311459 P/V/G.............................. $14.95

57. The 1960s
Beyond the Sea • Blue Velvet • California Dreamin' • Downtown • For Once in My Life • Let's Hang On • (Sittin' On) The Dock of the Bay • The Twist.
00311460 P/V/G.............................. $14.99

58. The 1970s
Dust in the Wind • Everything Is Beautiful • How Can You Mend a Broken Heart • I Feel the Earth Move • If • Joy to the World • My Eyes Adored You • You've Got a Friend.
00311461 P/V/G.............................. $14.99

61. Billy Joel Favorites
And So It Goes • Baby Grand • It's Still Rock and Roll to Me • Leave a Tender Moment Alone • Piano Man • She's Always a Woman • Uptown Girl • You May Be Right.
00311464 P/V/G.............................. $14.95

62. Billy Joel Hits
The Entertainer • Honesty • Just the Way You Are • The Longest Time • Lullabye (Goodnight, My Angel) • My Life • New York State of Mind • She's Got a Way.
00311465 P/V/G.............................. $14.95

63. High School Musical 2
All for One • Everyday • Fabulous • Gotta Go My Own Way • I Don't Dance • What Time Is It • Work This Out • You Are the Music in Me.
00311470 P/V/G.............................. $19.95

64. God Bless America
America • America, the Beautiful • Anchors Aweigh • Battle Hymn of the Republic • God Bless America • This Is My Country • This Land Is Your Land • and more.
00311489 P/V/G.............................. $14.95

65. Casting Crowns
Does Anybody Hear Her • East to West • Here I Go Again • Praise You in This Storm • Somewhere in the Middle • Voice of Truth • While You Were Sleeping • Who Am I.
00311494 P/V/G.............................. $14.95

66. Hannah Montana
I Got Nerve • Just like You • Life's What You Make It • Nobody's Perfect • Old Blue Jeans • Pumpin' up the Party • Rock Star • We Got the Party.
00311772 P/V/G.............................. $19.95

67. Broadway Gems
Getting to Know You • I Could Have Danced All Night • If I Were a Rich Man • It's a Lovely Day Today • September Song • The Song Is You • and more.
00311803 P/V/G.............................. $14.99

68. Lennon & McCartney Favorites
All My Loving • The Fool on the Hill • A Hard Day's Night • Here, There and Everywhere • I Saw Her Standing There • Yellow Submarine • and more.
00311804 P/V/G.............................. $14.95

69. Pirates of the Caribbean
All for One • Everyday • Fabulous • Gotta Go My Own Way • I Don't Dance • What Time Is It • Work This Out • You Are the Music in Me.
00311807 P/V/G.............................. $14.95

70. "Tomorrow," "Put on a Happy Face," And Other Charles Strouse Hits
Born Too Late • A Lot of Livin' to Do • Night Song • Once upon a Time • Put on a Happy Face • Those Were the Days • Tomorrow • You've Got Possibilities.
00311821 P/V/G.............................. $14.99

71. Rock Band
Black Hole Sun • Don't Fear the Reaper • Learn to Fly • Paranoid • Say It Ain't So • Suffragette City • Wanted Dead or Alive • Won't Get Fooled Again.
00311822 P/V/G.............................. $14.99

72. High School Musical 3
Can I Have This Dance • High School Musical • I Want It All • A Night to Remember • Now or Never • Right Here Right Now • Scream • Walk Away.
00311826 P/V/G.............................. $19.99

73. Mamma Mia! – The Movie
Dancing Queen • Gimme! Gimme! Gimme! (A Man After Midnight) • Honey, Honey • Lay All Your Love on Me • Mamma Mia • SOS • Take a Chance on Me • The Winner Takes It All.
00311831 P/V/G.............................. $14.99